W9-BYM-459

Quiz Master Football

by Michael Pellowski
illustrated by Tim Davis

**To football buddies
George Dumas and Jimmy Graves,
who are not forgotten**

First printing by Willowisp Press 1997.

Published by PAGES Publishing Group
801 94th Avenue North, St. Petersburg, Florida 33702

Willowisp Press®

Printed in the United States of America

2 4 6 8 10 9 7 5 3 1

ISBN 0 - 87406 - 870 - 3

Welcome,
football fans!

Enter the domain of the *QuizMaster* and test your knowledge of football trivia! Challenge your friends to a little scrimmage and see who has the best score at the end of the game.

Questions are scored according to difficulty:

1 point
These are easy gains.

2 points
Seasoned players should be able to score on these.

3 points
Only the most skilled players will tackle these questions.

Bonus Points
At the end of each quarter, you will have a chance to learn more fun facts for bonus points: these are the "point after" extra points that will help boost your score.

Answers can be found in the Answer Section beginning on page 67.

Good luck, sports fans! You're going to need it!

Let the game begin!

First Quarter

#1

Which NFL team won Super Bowl XXX, which was played in Tempe, Arizona, in January 1996?
(2 points)

Answer:

#2

Which college football bowl game is the oldest?
(1 point)

_____ a. the Orange Bowl

__X__ b. the Rose Bowl

_____ c. the Cotton Bowl

Total points possible: 3
My score: _____

#3

Who was the <u>first</u> college player to win the National Scoring
Title by scoring more than 200 points in a season?
(3 points)

Answer:

#4

Which NFL team did Dom Capers
coach during the 1996-97 season?
(2 points)

Answer:

Total points possible: 5
My score: _____

#5

Match the following NFL head coaches with the team each man coached in the 1996-97 season.
(1 point each)

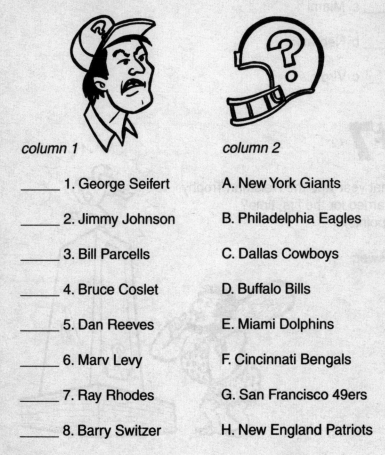

column 1

column 2

_____ 1. George Seifert

A. New York Giants

_____ 2. Jimmy Johnson

B. Philadelphia Eagles

_____ 3. Bill Parcells

C. Dallas Cowboys

_____ 4. Bruce Coslet

D. Buffalo Bills

_____ 5. Dan Reeves

E. Miami Dolphins

_____ 6. Marv Levy

F. Cincinnati Bengals

_____ 7. Ray Rhodes

G. San Francisco 49ers

_____ 8. Barry Switzer

H. New England Patriots

Total points possible: 8
My score: _____

#6

Which college team won the 1995 Orange Bowl game?
(1 point)

_____ a. Miami

_____ b. Nebraska

_____ c. Virginia

#7

What year was the Heisman Trophy awarded for the <u>first</u> time?
(2 points)

Answer:

Total points possible: 3
My score: _____

#8

Movie and TV star
Ed Marinaro played
professional football
and was an All-American
football star in college.
Which Ivy League
school did Marinaro attend?
(3 points)

Answer:

#9

Frank Filchock was the <u>first</u> NFL quarterback to throw a
99-yard touchdown pass. For which NFL team did
Filchock play when he tossed that TD pass?
(1 point)

_____ a. the Green Bay Packers

_____ b. the Chicago Bears

_____ c. the Washington Redskins

Total points possible: 4
My score: _____

#10

Which schools played in the first college
football game in history?
(3 points)

Answer:

#11

Dutch Clark is a member of the Professional Football Hall
of Fame. What position did Hall-of-Famer Clark play?
(2 points)

Answer:

Total points possible: 5
My score: _____

#12

How high is the crossbar
on a football goalpost?
(1 point)

_____ a. 8 feet high

_____ b. 10 feet high

_____ c. 12 feet high

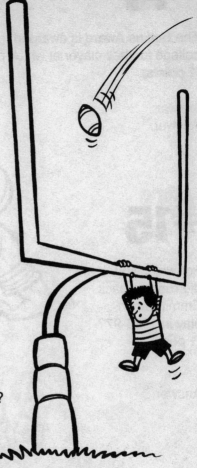

#13

How many players are
on a Canadian football team?
(3 points)

Answer:

Total points possible: 4
My score: _____

#14

The Butkus Award is awarded to the top college football player at which position?
(2 points)

Answer:

#15

For which NFL team did running back Emmitt Smith play in 1996-97?
(1 point)

Answer:

Total points possible: 3
My score: _____

#16

In which state in the U.S. is the Professional
Football Hall of Fame located?
(2 points)

Answer:

#17

Who was the first NFL runner to gain 1,000
yards rushing in his rookie season?
(3 points)

Answer:

Total points possible: 5
My score: _____

#18

For winning the 1933 NFL Championship, each member of the Championship Bears received <u>less</u> than $250.00 in bonus money.
(1 point)

_____ true

_____ false

#19

Who is considered the "Father of Football" for his many contributions to the sport?
(2 points)

_____ a. Walter Camp

_____ b. John Heisman

_____ c. Jim Thorpe

Total points possible: 3
My score: _____

#20

Penn State won its 700th career football game in 1996. What school did Penn State beat for its 700th career victory?
(3 points)

Answer:

Total points possible: 3
My score: _____

End of the First Quarter

(check your answers on pages 68 to 77)

Extra Points
from the
QuizMaster

Learn these five fun facts about football and add
five bonus points to your score!!

Extra Point #1:

The first college west of the Mississippi to play Yale in a game of football was the University of Iowa. Yale played Iowa in 1922 and won the game 6 to 0.

Extra Point #2:

The first player in NFL history to kick more than 20 field goals in a season was Lou "The Toe" Groza of the Cleveland Browns. Groza booted 23 field goals in 1953.

Extra Point #3:

A regulation football field in the United States measures 120 yards long and 53 1/3 yards wide.

Extra Point #4:

Al Hoisch of UCLA returned a kickoff a record 103 yards for a touchdown against the University of Illinois in the 1947 Rose Bowl.

Extra Point #5:

Bert Bell (who at the time was a co-owner of the Philadelphia Eagles) is credited with creating pro football's draft system in 1935.

Total score of correct first-quarter answers: _____ **(46 points possible)**

Plus five (5) bonus points: _____

Total score of the first quarter: _____

#21

The penalty flags used by officials in the National Football League have always been yellow.
(2 points)

_____ true

_____ false

Total points possible: 2
My score: _____

#22

Match each of the following cities with the NFL
team that plays in that city.
(2 points each)

column 1   *column 2*

_____ 1. Seattle   a. Ravens

_____ 2. Baltimore   b. Falcons

_____ 3. Atlanta   c. Seahawks

Total points possible: **6**
My score: _____

#23

Who was the first football player from Notre Dame
to win college football's Heisman Trophy?
(3 points)

Answer:

#24

How many times was quarterback Joe Montana voted
the Most Valuable Player (MVP) of the Super Bowl?
(2 points)

Answer:

Total points possible: 5
My score: _____

#25

The first Super Bowl was played in 1967. Which teams played in Super Bowl I <u>and</u> who won the game?
(3 points)

Answer:

#26

In football, is a safety man an offensive or defensive player?
(1 point)

Answer:

Total points possible: 4
My score: _____

#27

UCLA is a member of college football's Big Ten Conference.
(1 point)

_____ true

_____ false

#28

What number does
quarterback Troy Aikman
of the Dallas Cowboys wear?
(2 points)

Answer:

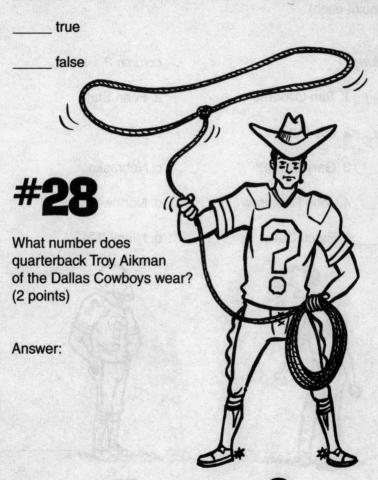

Total points possible: **3**
My score: _____

#29

Match the following football coaches with the college each one coached at in 1996-97:
(1 point each)

column 1   *column 2*

_____ 1. Tom Osborne   a. Penn State

_____ 2. Joe Paterno   b. USC

_____ 3. Gary Barnett   c. Nebraska

_____ 4. John Robinson   d. Northwestern

_____ 5. Butch Davis   e. Miami (Fla.)

Total points possible: 5
My score: _____

#30

Match the following former #1 draft picks in the NFL with the team each player was selected by. (2 points each)

column 1

_____ 1. Ki-Jana Carter (RB)

_____ 2. Russell Maryland (DL)

_____ 3. Irving Fryar (WR)

_____ 4. Bruce Smith (DE)

column 2

a. New England Patriots

b. Cincinnati Bengals

c. Buffalo Bills

d. Dallas Cowboys

Total points possible: 8
My score: _____

#31

Which of the following famous coaches won more football games in his college career?
(1 point)

_____ Glenn "Pop" Warner

_____ Paul "Bear" Bryant

#32

Who was the first African-American football player to win the Heisman Trophy?
(3 points)

Answer:

Total points possible: 4
My score: _____

#33

Who was the first NFL player to run 99 yards from the line
of scrimmage for a touchdown?
(3 points)

Answer:

#34

Sports announcer Frank Gifford played professional football for
which NFL team?
(2 points)

Answer:

Total points possible: 5
My score: _____

#35

Boise State, Montana, and
Idaho are all members of
which NCAA Division
I-AA Football Conference?
(2 points)

Answer:

#36

In a football game, how many points are awarded for a "safety"?
(1 point)

Answer:

Total points possible: 3
My score: _____

#37

Can you name four of the ten teams that make up
college football's Pac-10 Conference?
(1 point each)

1. _____

2. _____

3. _____

4. _____

Total points possible: **4**
My score: _____

#38

Who kicked the longest field goal ever recorded in the history of the National Football League?
(3 points)

Answer:

#39

Football helmets have always had face masks on them.
(1 point)

_____ true

_____ false

Total points possible: 4
My score: _____

#40

Who was the first player in the NFL to return a punt
103 yards for a touchdown?
(2 points)

_____ a. Robert Bailey

_____ b. Charlie West

_____ c. Dennis Morgan

Total points possible: 2
My score: _____

End of the Second Quarter

(check your answers on pages 78 to 90)

Extra Points
from the
QuizMaster

Learn these five fun facts about basketball and add
five bonus points to your score!!

Extra Point #1:

The area on the field where the football lies is called the neutral zone. The neutral zone is from one tip of the ball to the other.

Extra Point #2:

The Flying Wedge, a dangerous power-blocking formation that caused many serious injuries, was outlawed from football in 1894.

Extra Point #3:
In Canadian football, the offensive team has only three downs to advance the ball ten yards for a first down.

Extra Point #4:
The first All-America Football Team was selected in 1889.

Extra Point #5:
The Seattle Seahawks and the Tampa Bay Buccaneers entered the NFL in 1976.

Total score of correct second-quarter answers: _____ (54 points possible)

Plus five (5) bonus points: _____

Total score of the second quarter: _____

#41

What is the name of the trophy awarded to the champions
of the Canadian Football League (CFL)?
(2 points)

Answer:

Total points possible: 2
My score: _____

#42

Match each of the following Canadian cities with the correct
Canadian football team that plays there.
(1 point each)

column 1   *column 2*

_____ 1. Toronto   a. Tiger-Cats

_____ 2. Calgary   b. Stampeders

_____ 3. Hamilton   c. Argonauts

#43

Which coach won more
NFL games during his
coaching career?
(1 point)

_____ John Madden

_____ Vince Lombardi

Total points possible: 4
My score: _____

#44

NBA basketball star Grant Hill is the son of Calvin Hill, a great NFL running back.
(1 point)

_____ true

_____ false

#45

How deep is the end zone of an official football field in the United States?
(2 points)

Answer: _____ yards

Total points possible: 3
My score: _____

#46

Can you name four of the eight schools that are members
of college football Ivy League?
(1 point each)

1. _____

2. _____

3. _____

4. _____

#47

Which <u>two</u> NFL teams did quarterback
Joe Montana play for during his
pro football career?
(1 point each)

1. _____

2. _____

Total points possible: 6
My score: _____

#48

In which state in the U.S. is college football's
Sugar Bowl played?
(1 point)

Answer

#49

Al Carmichael was the first player in NFL history to return a
kickoff 106 yards for a touchdown. Which team did Carmichael
play for when he made that record kickoff return in 1956?
(1 point)

_____ New York Giants

_____ Chicago Bears

_____ Green Bay Packers

Total points possible: 2
My score: _____

#50

How many officials are there in a college football game?
(2 points)

Answer:

#51

Which team won the most NFL championships
from 1960 to 1969?
(1 point)

_____ Green Bay Packers

_____ Minnesota Vikings

_____ Dallas Cowboys

Total points possible: 3
My score: _____

#52

Jim Thorpe, one of football's greatest players, was a Native American from the Sac and Fox tribe.
(1 point)

_____ true

_____ false

#53

Harold "Red" Grange played running back for the University of Illinois during the 1920s and is a member of College Football's Hall of Fame. What is Red Grange's famous nickname?
(2 points)

_____ a. The Galloping Ghost

_____ b. The Wild Rhino

_____ c. The Streak of Smoke

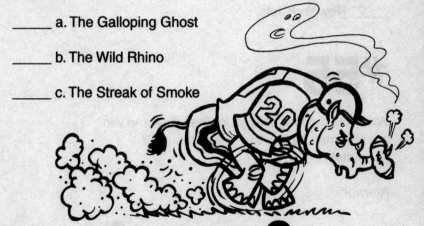

Total points possible: 3
My score: _____

#54

Which American Football Conference (AFC) franchise
of the NFL is older?
(1 point)

_____ Miami Dolphins

_____ New York Jets

#55

Who was the first college football player to win
the Heisman Trophy two years in a row?
(3 points)

Answer:

Total points possible: 4
My score: _____

#56

Who was the first player in the NFL <u>or</u> AFL to catch
100 passes in a single season?
(3 points)

Answer:

#57

Running back Dick Kazmaier was the last football player
from the Ivy League to win the Heisman Trophy.
Which Ivy League school did Kazmaier play for?
(3 points)

Answer:

Total points possible: 6
My score: _____

#58

Match each of the following members of the College Football Hall of Fame with the school each star played for.
(2 points each)

column 1

_____ 1. Sammy Baugh (QB)

_____ 2. Ernie Nevers (FB)

_____ 3. Bronko Nagurski (FB/T)

_____ 4. Sid Luckman (QB)

_____ 5. Byron "Whizzer" White (RB)

column 2

a. Stanford University

b. University of Minnesota

c. Columbia University

d. Texas Christian University

e. University of Colorado

Total points possible: 10

My score: _____

#59

President John F. Kennedy played varsity football at Harvard University during the 1930s.
(1 point)

_____ true

_____ false

#60

Match each of the following schools with its correct sports nickname.
(1 point each)

column 1   column 2

_____ 1. Michigan State   a. Cornhuskers

_____ 2. Auburn   b. Tigers

_____ 3. Nebraska   c. Spartans

Total points possible: 4
My score: _____

End of the
Third Quarter

(check your answers on pages 91 to 101)

Extra Points
from the
QuizMaster

Learn these five fun facts about football and add
five bonus points to your score!!

Extra
Point #1:

When the New York Jets played in
the American Football League in
the early 1960s, the team was
known as the New York Titans.

Extra
Point #2:

In 1987 a strike staged by NFL
players lasted for 24 days and
shortened the NFL season
from 16 games to 15 games.

Extra Point #3:
Football Hall-of-Famer Bronislaw Nagurski was better known by his famous nickname "Bronko."

Extra Point #4:
In 1933, the cost of an NFL franchise was a mere $10,000.

Extra Point #4:
Yale coach Walter Camp is the man who invented the position of quarterback.

Total score of correct third-quarter answers: _____ **(49 points possible)**

Plus five (5) bonus points: _____

Total score of the third quarter: _____

Fourth Quarter

#61

Match the following NFL quarterbacks with the number each one wears and the team each one played for in 1996. (1 point each)

	Number	Team	
John Elway	_____	_____	1. #13
Neil O'Donnell	_____	_____	2. #4
Dan Marino	_____	_____	3. #7
Rick Mirer	_____	_____	4. #8
Jim Harbaugh	_____	_____	5. #14
Steve Young	_____	_____	6. #3

a. Seattle Seahawks   d. New York Jets

b. Miami Dolphins   e. San Francisco 49ers

c. Indianapolis Colts   f. Denver Broncos

Total points possible: 12
My score: _____

#62

Match the following NFL coaches with the correct number of victories each one posted during his career.
(2 points each)

column 1

_____ 1. Joe Gibbs (12 years)

_____ 2. Don Coryell (14 years)

_____ 3. Mike Ditka (11 years)

column 2

a. 112 victories

b. 140 victories

c. 114 victories

Total points possible: 6
My score: _____

#63

In which year was the American Professional Football Association renamed the National Football League (NFL)?
(1 point)

_____ 1908

_____ 1922

_____ 1928

#64

Who was the first running back in the NFL to capture the league's rushing title by gaining more than 1,500 yards in a single season?
(3 points)

Answer:

Total points possible: 4
My score: _____

#65

In which year did the National Football League hold
its very first NFL draft?
(2 points)

Answer:

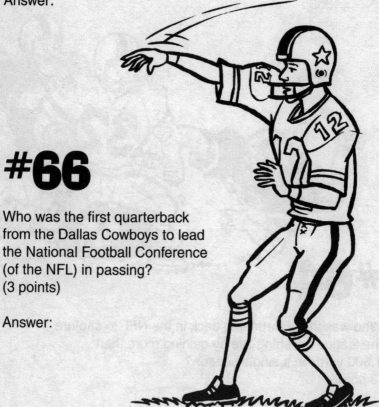

#66

Who was the first quarterback
from the Dallas Cowboys to lead
the National Football Conference
(of the NFL) in passing?
(3 points)

Answer:

Total points possible: 5
My score: _____

#67

Before becoming a coach at Notre Dame, football immortal Knute Rockne was a star quarterback for the University of Notre Dame.
(1 point)

_____ true   _____ false

#68

Who is the all-time leading rusher in NFL history?
(3 points)

Answer:

Total points possible: 4
My score: _____

#69

How many times was
Gale Sayers voted
the Most Valuable Back
in the NFL Pro Bowl?
(2 points)

Answer:

#70

Coach John Heisman won more college football games
during his career than Coach Vince Dooley did during
his college career.
(1 point)

_____ true

_____ false

Total points possible: 3
My score: _____

#71

Has Brigham Young University ever been declared
the National Champion of college football?
(2 points)

_____ yes

_____ no

#72

Which college football team has appeared in more
post-season bowl games than any other school?
(3 points)

Answer:

Total points possible: 5
My score: _____

#73

Match the following pro coaches with the Super-Bowl-winning team each man coached and the correct Super Bowl title his team won.
(1 point each)

	Team	Super Bowl
1. Hank Stram	_____	_____
2. John Madden	_____	_____
3. Weeb Ewbank	_____	_____

    1. Oakland Raiders   a. Super Bowl IV
    2. Kansas City Chiefs   b. Super Bowl III
    3. New York Jets   c. Super Bowl XI

Total points possible: 6
My score: _____

#74

Which NFL team scored the fewest points ever
in a Super Bowl?
(3 points)

Answer:

#75

In which U. S. state was the 1996 NFL Pro Bowl played?
(2 points)

Answer:

Total points possible: 5
My score: _____

#76

Willie Davis and Jim Ringo are both members of Pro Football's Hall of Fame. Which one of them was an offensive center?
(1 point)

Answer:

#77

In what year was the first NFL Pro Bowl played?
(2 points)

Answer:

Total points possible: 3
My score: _____

#78

In a football game, a defensive "nose tackle" normally lines up opposite which offensive lineman?
(2 points)

Answer:

Total points possible: 2
My score: _____

#79

Who was the first person to be named the Most Valuable Player in the Super Bowl who was not a quarterback?
(3 points)

Answer:

Total points possible: 3
My score: _____

#80

Match the following college football all-stars with the year
each one won the Heisman Trophy.
(2 points each)

column 1   *column 2*

_____ 1. Doug Flutie (Boston College)   a. 1993

_____ 2. Charlie Ward (Florida State)   b. 1981

_____ 3. Marcus Allen (USC)   c. 1994

_____ 4. Rashaan Salaam (Colorado)   d. 1984

Total points possible: 8
My score: _____

End of the Fourth Quarter

(check your answers on pages 102 to 111)

Extra Points
from the
QuizMaster

Learn these five fun facts about football and add
five bonus points to your score!!

Extra Point #1:

A football weighs between 14 and 15 ounces and is inflated to an air pressure of between 12 1/2 and 13 1/2 pounds per square inch.

Extra Point #2:

Politician Jack Kemp formerly played pro football as a quarterback and threw 114 TD passes during his NFL career.

Extra Point #3:
The Outland Trophy is awarded annually to the outstanding lineman in college football.

Extra Point #4:
Joe Rizzo was the first graduate of the U.S. Merchant Marine Academy to play football in the NFL.

Extra Point #5:
A team named the Brooklyn Dodgers played in the NFL in 1926.

Total score of correct fourth-quarter answers: _____ **(66 points possible)**

Plus five (5) bonus points: _____

Total score of the fourth quarter: _____

5...4...3...2....1.....

Game over!

Now add up all your scores:

First quarter score: _____

Second quarter score: _____

Third quarter score: _____

Fourth quarter score: _____

Grand Total: _____

QuizMaster Ranking

190-235 points   MVP
(Mega-Valuable Player)

140-189 points   SVP
(Semi-Valuable Player)

90-139 points   RPM
(Relief Player Material)

40-89 points   PIT
(Player-in-Training)

Thanks for playing!
Now, shake hands and
hit the lockers!

The QuizMaster Tells All!!!

Quarter-by-Quarter
ANSWERS

First Quarter Answers

from page 5

#1

The Dallas Cowboys won Super Bowl XXX. The Cowboys captured the Super Bowl crown in 1996 by defeating the Pittsburgh Steelers 27 to 17 in Tempe, Arizona. (2 points)

#2

The answer is **b**, the Rose Bowl. The first Rose Bowl game was played in 1902. The first Orange Bowl game took place in 1933, and the first Cotton Bowl contest was held in 1937. (1 point)

from page 6

#3

Barry Sanders. Running back Barry Sanders of Oklahoma State won the National Scoring Title in 1988, scoring 234 points for a 21.3 points-per-game average. Sanders is now an NFL star. (3 points)

#4

The Carolina Panthers. (2 points)

from page 7

#5

1. g   (George Seifert-San Francisco 49ers)
2. e   (Jimmy Johnson-Miami Dolphins)
3. h   (Bill Parcells-New England Patriots)
4. f   (Bruce Coslet-Cincinnati Bengals)
5. a   (Dan Reeves-New York Giants)
6. d   (Marv Levy-Buffalo Bills)
7. b   (Ray Rhodes-Philadelphia Eagles)
8. c   (Barry Switzer-Dallas Cowboys)

(1 point for each correct answer)

#6

Nebraska. Nebraska won the 1995 Orange Bowl, defeating Miami 24 to 17. Nebraska posted a 12-0 record with the win on January 1st and captured the National Championship. Virginia won the Independence Bowl during the 1994-95 season. (1 point)

#7

1935. The first Heisman Trophy (awarded to the Outstanding College Football Player in the U.S.) was awarded to Jay Berwanger of the University of Chicago in 1935. (2 points)

from page 9

#8

Cornell University. Ed Marinaro was an All-American running back for Cornell during the 1970s. (3 points)

#9

The answer is **c**, the Washington Redskins. On October 15, 1939, quarterback Frank Filchock of the Redskins completed a 99-yard touchdown pass to end Andy Farkas in a game against the Pittsburgh Steelers. (1 point)

from page 10

#10

Rutgers University and Princeton University. Rutgers played Princeton in the first college football game in history on November 6, 1869, at New Brunswick, New Jersey, the site of the Rutgers campus. Rutgers won the first college football game by defeating Princeton 6 goals to 4 goals. (3 points)

#11

Quarterback. Dutch Clark was a quarterback, first for the Portsmouth Spartans and then for the Detroit Lions, from 1931 to 1938. (2 points)

#12

The answer is **b**, 10 feet high. The crossbar on a football goal post measures 10 feet high from the ground. (1 point)

#13

Twelve (12). Football teams in Canada use 12 players on a side. On offense, the extra player usually lines up in the backfield. On defense, the extra player is usually a linebacker or a defensive back. (3 points)

from page 12

#14

Linebacker. The Butkus Award was established in 1985 by the Downtown Athletic Club of Orlando and is named for College Hall-of-Famer Dick Butkus of Illinois. (2 points)

#15

The Dallas Cowboys. In 1996 running back Emmitt Smith signed a $48 million, 8-year contract with the Cowboys, which included a $15 million signing bonus. (1 point)

from page 13

#16

Ohio. The Pro Football Hall of Fame is located in Canton, Ohio. It was established in 1962. (2 points)

#17

Beattie Feathers. In 1934 rookie Beattie Feathers of the Chicago Bears rushed for 1,004 yards in 13 NFL games.   (3 points)

#18

True. When the Bears beat the New York Giants 23 to 21 in the 1933 NFL Championship, each member of the Bears received $210.34 in bonus money. Each member of the second-place Giants team received $140.22 in bonus money. (1 point)

#19

The answer is **a**, Walter Camp. Walter Camp is considered to be the Father of Football. Camp played football at Yale, and later made important contributions to the sport. Walt Camp came up with the ideas to start play from a line of scrimmage and to use a series of downs to advance the ball. (2 points)

from page 15

#20

Wisconsin. Penn State edged Wisconsin 23 to 20 to earn its 700th career gridiron victory on September 28, 1996. (3 points)

End of First Quarter Answers

from
page
19

#21

False. The penalty flags used in the National Football League were originally white. It wasn't until 1965 that the NFL changed the color of penalty flags from white to yellow. (2 points)

from page 20

#22

1. c (Seattle Seahawks)

2. a (Baltimore Ravens)

3. b (Atlanta Falcons)

(2 points for each correct answer)

from page 21

#23

Angelo Bertelli. Quarterback Angelo Bertelli became the first Heisman Trophy winner from Notre Dame when he won the award in 1943. (3 points)

#24

Three (3) times. Quarterback Joe Montana was voted the MVP of Super Bowl XVI, Super Bowl XIX, and Super Bowl XXIV. (2 points)

#25

The Green Bay Packers and the Kansas City Chiefs met in Super Bowl I. The Packers won by the score of 35-10.   (3 points)

#26

A defensive player. The safety men are defensive backs who help cover the middle of the field. The strong safety usually lines up on the tight end, while the free safety is free to go to the ball. (1 point)

#27

False. UCLA is a member of college football's Pacific-10 (PAC-10) Conference. (1 point)

#28

QB Troy Aikman of the Dallas Cowboys wears the number 8. (2 points)

from page 24

#29

1. c (Tom Osborne-Nebraska)

2. a (Joe Paterno-Penn State)

3. d (Gary Barnett-Northwestern)

4. b (John Robinson-USC)

5. e (Butch Davis-Miami of Fla.)

(1 point for each correct answer)

from page 25

#30

1. b (Ki-Jana Carter, RB, Cincinnati Bengals)

2. d (Russell Maryland, DL, Dallas Cowboys)

3. a (Irving Fryar, WR, New England Patriots)

4. c (Bruce Smith, DE, Buffalo Bills)

(2 points for each correct answer)

from page 26

#31

Paul "Bear" Bryant. Bear Bryant won 323 football games during his college coaching career, whereas Glenn "Pop" Warner won 319 football games during his college career. (1 point)

#32

Ernie Davis. Running back Ernie Davis of Syracuse won the Heisman Trophy as the Outstanding College Football Player in the U.S. in 1961. (3 points)

#33

Tony Dorsett. Tony Dorsett of the Dallas Cowboys ran 99 yards from the line of scrimmage to score a touchdown against the Minnesota Vikings on January 3, 1983. (3 points)

#34

The New York Giants. Frank Gifford played pro football as a back for the New York Giants from 1952 to 1960 and then from 1962 to 1964. (2 points)

from
page
28

#35

The Big Sky Conference. (2 points)

#36

A safety is worth two (2) points. (1 point)

from page 29

#37

Members of the PAC-10 Football Conference are:

UCLA
Oregon
Arizona
Washington
Washington State
USC
California
Oregon State
Stanford
Arizona State

(1 point for each correct answer)

from page 30

#38

Tom Dempsey. Tom Dempsey of the New Orleans Saints booted an NFL-record 63-yard field goal against the Detroit Lions on November 8, 1970. (3 points)

#39

False. Early football helmets were made of leather (not plastic) and did <u>not</u> have face masks on them. (1 point)

from page 31

#40

The answer is **a**, Robert Bailey. Robert Bailey of the Los Angeles Rams returned a punt 103 yards for a touchdown against the New Orleans Saints on October 23, 1994. Charlie West and Dennis Morgan both returned punts 98 yards for scores during their NFL careers. (2 points)

End of Second Quarter Answers

from
page
35

#**41**

The Grey Cup. The Grey Cup, originally donated by Earl Grey (a former Governor-General of Canada), has been awarded to the winner of the Canadian Football League's Championship Game since 1954. (2 points)

from page 36

#42

1. c (Toronto Argonauts)

2. b (Calgary Stampeders)

3. a (Hamilton Tiger-Cats)

(1 point for each correct answer)

#43

John Madden. John Madden won 112 games and lost 39 games during his coaching career, whereas Vince Lombardi won 105 games and lost 35 games during his career (including playoff games). (1 point)

from
page
37

#44

True. Grant Hill, who plays in the NBA, is the son of NFL-great Calvin Hill. Calvin Hill was a star running back for the Dallas Cowboys and was the NFL's Rookie of the Year in 1969. (1 point)

#45

Ten (10) yards deep. The end zone of an official football field in the U.S. measures ten yards from the goal line to the end line. (2 points)

from page 38

#46

Members of college football's Ivy League are:

Princeton
Penn
Brown
Cornell
Columbia
Yale
Harvard
Dartmouth

(1 point for each correct answer)

#47

The San Francisco 49ers and the Kansas City Chiefs. Joe Montana played 14 years with the San Francisco 49ers, leading them to four Super Bowl crowns. He played for the Kansas City Chiefs during his last two years in the NFL. (1 point for each correct answer)

#48

Louisiana. The Sugar Bowl is played in New Orleans, Louisiana. The first Sugar Bowl contest was held in 1935. In that game, Tulane beat Temple 20 to 14 to win the first Sugar Bowl contest. (1 point)

#49

The Green Bay Packers. Al Carmichael of the Green Bay Packers returned a kickoff 106 yards for a touchdown against the Chicago Bears on October 7, 1956. (1 point)

from page 40

#50

Six (6). There are six (6) officials in a college football game. They are the referee, the umpire, the linesman, the field judge, the back judge, and the timekeeper (or clock operator). (2 points)

#51

The Green Bay Packers. The Packers won five (5) NFL Championships from 1960 to 1969. Green Bay captured NFL crowns in 1961, 1962, 1965, 1966, and 1967. (1 point)

from page 41

#52

True. Jim Thorpe was a member of the Sac and Fox Tribe and his Native American name, "Iwa-Tho-Huck," means "Bright Path." Jim Thorpe is a member of both the College and Pro Football Halls of Fame. (1 point)

#53

The answer is **a**, The Galloping Ghost. Harold "Red" Grange was nicknamed the Galloping Ghost because of his elusive style of broken field running. (2 points)

from
page
42

#54

The New York Jets. The Jets played their first season in 1960, whereas the Miami Dolphins played their first season in 1966. Both teams were originally members of the American Football League before the AFL merged with the NFL. (1 point)

#55

Archie Griffin. Running back Archie Griffin of Ohio State won the Heisman Trophy in 1974 and in 1975. (3 points)

from page 43

#56

Lionel Taylor of the AFL's Denver Broncos. In 1961 Lionel Taylor of the Broncos caught 100 passes to lead the AFL in receptions. (3 points)

#57

Princeton. Halfback Dick Kazmaier of Princeton University won the Heisman Trophy in 1951. (2 points)

from page 44

#58

1. d (Sammy Baugh, QB, Texas Christian University)
2. a (Ernie Nevers, FB, Stanford Universiy)
3. b (Bronko Nagurski, FB/T, University of Minnesota)
4. c (Sid Luckman, QB, Columbia University)
5. e (Byron "Whizzer" White, HB, University of Colorado)

(2 points for each correct answer)

from
page
45

#59

False. President John F. Kennedy did not play varsity football at Harvard. He did play end at Harvard on the freshman and JV football squads during the 1930s.
(1 point)

#60

1. c (Michigan State Spartans)

2. b (Auburn Tigers)

3. a (Nebraska Cornhuskers)

(1 point for each correct answer)

End of Third Quarter Answers

from page 49

#61

1. 3, f   John Elway (#7, Denver Broncos)

2. 5, d   Neil O'Donnell (#14, New York Jets)

3. 1, b   Dan Marino (#13, Miami Dolphins)

4. 6, a   Rick Mirer (#3, Seattle Seahawks)

5. 2, c   Jim Harbaugh (#4, Indianapolis Colts)

6. 4, e   Steve Young (#8, San Francisco 49ers)

(1 point for each correct answer)

#62

1. b (Joe Gibbs: 12 years, 140 victories)

2. c (Don Coryell: 14 years, 114 victories)

3. a (Mike Ditka: 11 years, 112 victories)

(2 points for each correct answer)

#63

The answer is **1922**. (2 points)

#64

Jim Brown. Running back Jim Brown of the Cleveland Browns gained 1,527 yards in 1958 to lead the NFL in rushing. Jim Brown led the NFL in rushing eight (8) times from 1957 to 1965. In 1963 he rushed for 1,863 yards, and in 1965 he rushed for 1,544 yards. (3 points)

from page 52

#65

1936. The first National Football League draft was held in 1936. The first player drafted in 1936 was Heisman Trophy winner Jay Berwanger, who decided not to play pro football for the Philadelphia Eagles. (2 points)

#66

Roger Staubach. Quarterback Roger Staubach of the Dallas Cowboys led the NFL in passing in 1973 and also in 1977, 1978, and 1979. He was the first Cowboy QB to earn that honor. (3 points)

from page 53

#67

False. Knute Rockne was a star player for Notre Dame during the early 1900s, but he was an end, not a quarter-back. The QB of the team Rockne played on was Charles "Gus" Dorais. (1 point)

#68

Walter Payton. Walter Payton of the Chicago Bears is the NFL's all-time leading rusher. In 13 years Payton gained 16,726 yards on 3,838 carries for an average of 4.4 yards per carry. (3 points)

from
page
54

#69

Three (3) times. Gale Sayers of the Chicago Bears won the MVP Award as the best back in the NFL Pro Bowl in 1967, 1968, and 1970. (2 points)

#70

False. Coach John Heisman won 185 games during his 36-year college coaching career, whereas Vince Dooley won 201 games during his 25-year college coaching career.   (1 point)

from page 55

#71

Yes. Brigham Young University (BYU) was declared the National Champion of College Football when it posted a perfect 13-0 record in 1984. (1 point)

#72

Alabama. The University of Alabama has appeared in more post-season bowls than any other school. (2 points)

from page
56

#73

1. 2, a   Hank Stram (Kansas City Chiefs, Super Bowl IV)

2. 1, c   John Madden (Oakland Raiders, Super Bowl XI)

3. 3, b   Weeb Ewbank (New York Jets, Super Bowl III)

(1 point for each correct answer)

from page 57

#74

The Miami Dolphins. The Dolphins only scored three (3) points in Super Bowl VI. The Dallas Cowboys beat Miami 24-3 in Super Bowl VI, which was played on January 16, 1972. (3 points)

#75

Hawaii. The 1996 NFL Pro Bowl was held in Hawaii. In the contest, the NFC All-Stars edged the AFC All-Stars 20 to 13. (2 points)

from
page
58

#76

Jim Ringo. Ringo played offensive center for the Green Bay Packers and the Philadelphia Eagles. Willie Davis was a defensive end for the Green Bay Packers. (1 point)

#77

1951. The first NFL Pro Bowl was played in 1951 and it was won by the American Conference All-Stars by the score of 28 to 27. The MVP of the contest was quarterback Otto Graham of the Cleveland Browns. (2 points)

from
page
59

#78

The center. A nose tackle normally lines up against the offensive center. (2 points)

from page 60

#79

Chuck Howley. Linebacker Chuck Howley of the Dallas Cowboys was named the MVP of Super Bowl V. Until then, every previous MVP of the Super Bowl had played quarterback. (3 points)

from page 61

#80

1. d   Doug Flutie: Boston College, 1984

2. a   Charlie Ward: Florida State, 1993

3. b   Marcus Allen: USC, 1981

4. c   Rashaan Salaam: Colorado, 1994

(2 points for each correct answer)

End of Fourth Quarter Answers

Game Over!
The QuizMaster has left the stadium.